HAL•LEONARD

UKULELE
PLAY-ALONG

AUDIO
ACCESS
INCLUDED

PLAYBACK+
Speed • Pitch • Balance • Loop

arley

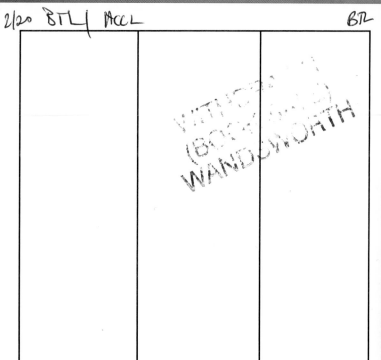

To access audio visit:
www.halleonard.com/mylibrary

Enter Code
2030-1601-7962-8675

Photo courtesy Photofest
Ukulele by Chris Kringel

ISBN 978-1-4768-7558-3

D1428688

HAL•LEONARD®
CORPORATION
7777 W. BLUEMOUND RD. P.O. BOX 13819 MILWAUKEE, WI 53213

9030 00007 0308 9

UKULELE NOTATION LEGEND

THE MUSICAL STAFF shows pitches and rhythms and is divided by bar lines into measures. Pitches are named after the first seven letters of the alphabet.

TABLATURE graphically represents the ukulele fingerboard. Each horizontal line represents a a string, and each number represents a fret.

2nd string, 3rd fret | 1st & 2nd strings open, played together | open F chord

HALF-STEP BEND: Strike the note and bend up 1/2 step.

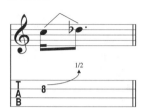

WHOLE-STEP BEND: Strike the note and bend up one step.

GRACE NOTE BEND: Strike the note and immediately bend up as indicated.

SLIGHT (MICROTONE) BEND: Strike the note and bend up 1/4 step.

BEND AND RELEASE: Strike the note and bend up as indicated, then release back to the original note. Only the first note is struck.

PRE-BEND: Bend the note as indicated, then strike it.

VIBRATO: The string is vibrated by rapidly bending and releasing the note with the fretting hand.

HAMMER-ON: Strike the first (lower) note with one finger, then sound the higher note (on the same string) with another finger by fretting it without picking.

PULL-OFF: Place both fingers on the notes to be sounded. Strike the first note and without picking, pull the finger off to sound the second (lower) note.

LEGATO SLIDE: Strike the first note and then slide the same fret-hand finger up or down to the second note. The second note is not struck.

SHIFT SLIDE: Same as legato slide, except the second note is struck.

TRILL: Very rapidly alternate between the notes indicated by continuously hammering on and pulling off.

TREMOLO PICKING: The note is picked as rapidly and continuously as possible.

NOTE: Tablature numbers in parentheses mean:

1. The note is being sustained over a system (note in standard notation is tied), or

2. The note is sustained, but a new articulation (such as a hammer-on, pull-off, slide or vibrato) begins, or

3. The note is a barely audible "ghost" note (note in standard notation is also in parentheses).

Additional Musical Definitions

 *(accent)* • Accentuate note (play it louder)

 (staccato) • Play the note short

D.S. al Coda • Go back to the sign (𝄋), then play until the measure marked "***To Coda***," then skip to the section labelled "**Coda.**"

D.C. al Fine • Go back to the beginning of the song and play until the measure marked "***Fine***" (end).

N.C. • No chord.

• Repeat measures between signs.

| 1. | 2. | • When a repeated section has different endings, play the first ending only the first time and the second ending only the second time.

Could You Be Loved

Words and Music by Bob Marley

TRACK 1

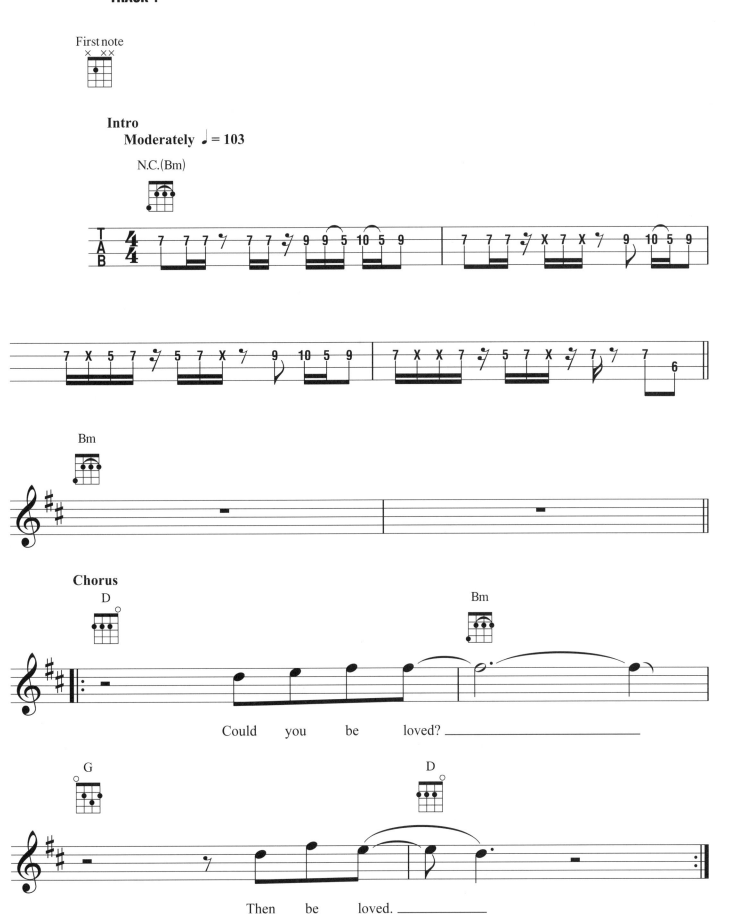

Verse

Bm

1. Don't let them fool ___ ya,
2. Don't let them change _ ya, oh,

Em

Bm

or e - ven try to school _ ya.
or e - ven re - ar - range _ ya.

Em

Oh, _____ no.
Oh, _____ no.

Bm

We've got a mind of our own. ___ So, go
We've got a life to live. ___

G   F#m   Em

to hell if what you think - in' is not right. _____
They say ___

Love __ would nev - er leave us a - lone. _____ Ah, in
On - ly, _____ on - ly, _____ on - ly

To Coda ⊕

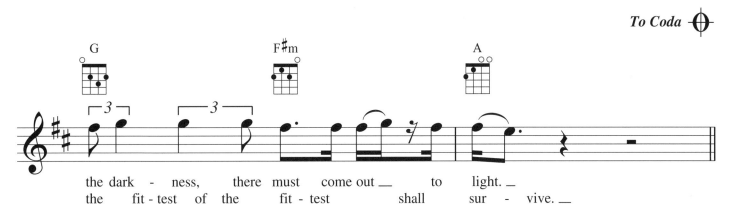

the dark - ness, there must come out __ to light. __
the fit - test of the fit - test shall sur - vive. __

Chorus

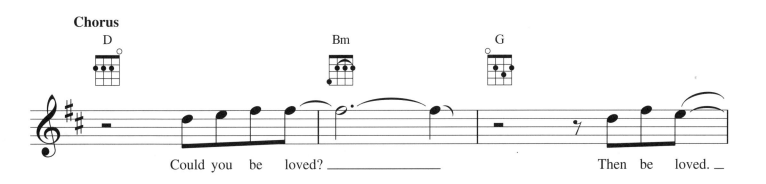

Could you be loved? _____ Then be loved. __

_____ Now, could you be loved? _____ Whoa, __

___ yeah. Then be loved. _____

Bridge

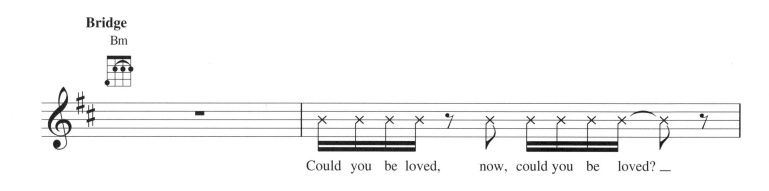

Could you be loved, now, could you be loved? __

The

road of life is rock - y and you may stum - ble, too. __ So,

why don't you point your fin - gers at some-one else that's judg-ing you. Love __

__ your bro - ther, man. __
(Could you be, could you be, could you be loved? Could you be, could you be loved?

D.S. al Coda

Could you be, could you be, could you be loved? Could you be, could you be loved?

Coda

Chorus

Stay a - live. ___   Eh. ___   Could you be loved? _____

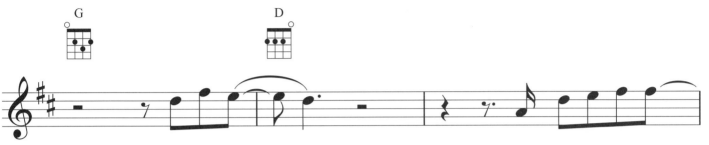

Then be loved. _____   Now, could you be loved? _

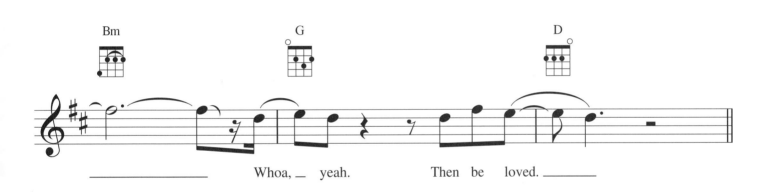

_____   Whoa, _ yeah.   Then be loved. _____

Outro
    w/ Voc. ad lib.
    Bm

Play 10 times

Begin fade   *Fade out*

Get Up Stand Up

Words and Music by Bob Marley and Peter Tosh

Intro

Moderately slow ♩ = 78

N.C.(B♭)

Get up, stand up. Stand up for ___ your right.

Get up, stand up.
{ 1. Stand up for ___ your right. }
{ 2., 3. Don't give up ___ the fight. }

Get up, stand up. Stand up for ___ your right.

To Coda ⊕

Get up, stand up. Don't give up ___ the fight.

Verse

1. Preach-er man don't tell ____ me __ heav-en is un - der the earth. __
2. Most peo - ple think great God will come from the sky, __

I know you don't know what life is real - ly worth. He said all __
take a - way ev-'ry-thing and make __ ev-'ry-bod-y feel high.

____ that glit-ter is gold. __ Half that sto - ry ain't nev - er been told. __ So
But if you know what life is worth you will look for yours on earth. And

2nd time, D.S. al Coda

now you see ____ the light, _ eh. You stand up for ____ your right. Come on!
now you see ____ the light. You stand up for ____ your right. Jah!

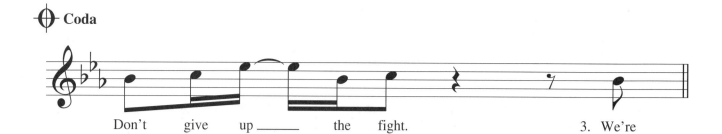
Coda

Don't give up _____ the fight. 3. We're

Verse

Cm

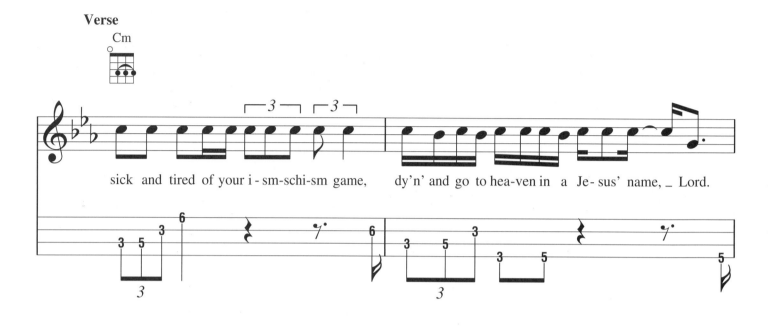

sick and tired of your i-sm-schi-sm game, dy'n' and go to hea-ven in a Je-sus' name, _ Lord.

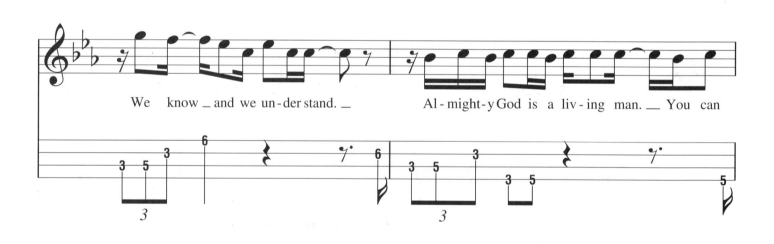

We know _ and we un-der stand. _ Al-might-y God is a liv-ing man. _ You can

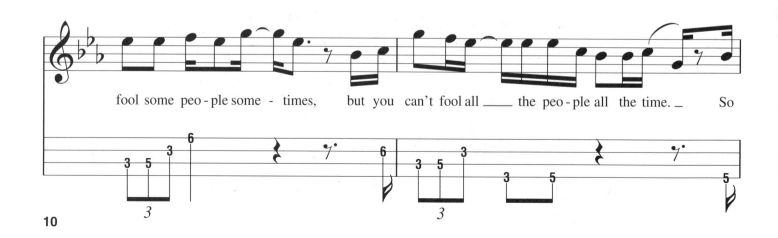

fool some peo-ple some - times, but you can't fool all _____ the peo-ple all the time. _ So

10

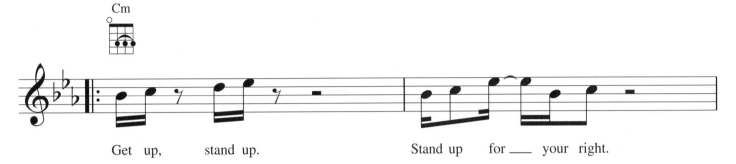

Outro-Chorus

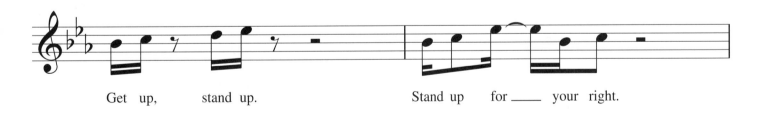

TRACK 5

I Shot the Sheriff

Words and Music by Bob Marley

First note

Chorus

Moderately slow ♩ = 96

(I shot the sher - iff but I did - n't shoot no

1. 2.

dep - u - ty. { Oh, no, _____ oh. _____   Yeah. _____
{ Oo, oo, _ _____ ooh.)

Verse

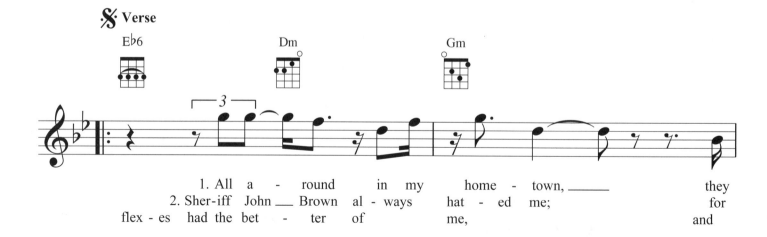

1. All a - round in my home - town, _____ they
2. Sher - iff John _____ Brown al - ways hat - ed me; for
flex - es had the bet - ter of me, and

try - in' ____ to track me down, ___ yeah. ___ They
what, _ I don't know. _____ Ev - 'ry
what is to be must be. Ev - 'ry

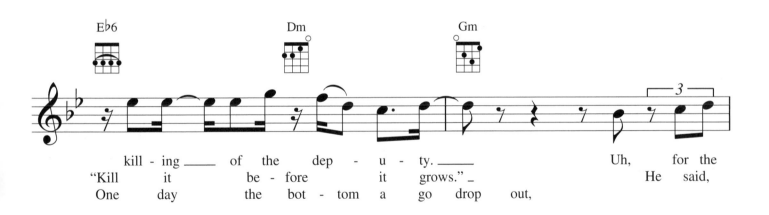

say they want to bring me ____ in guilt - y _____ for the
time I plant a seed, _____ he said,
day the buck - et a go a well. _____

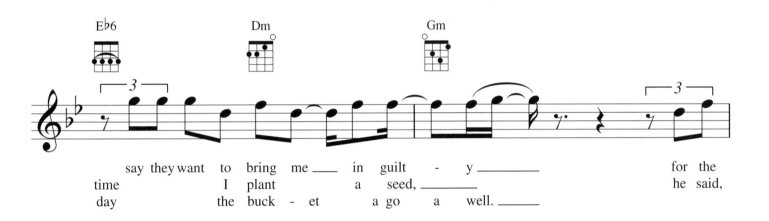

kill - ing ____ of the dep - u - ty. _____ Uh, for the
"Kill it be - fore it grows." _ He said,
One day the bot - tom a go drop out,

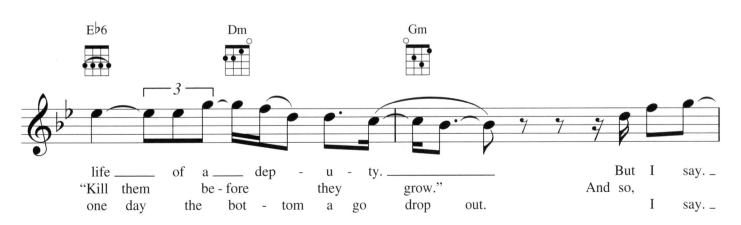

life _____ of a ____ dep - u - ty. _____ But I say. _
"Kill them be - fore they grow." And so,
one day the bot - tom a go drop out. I say. _

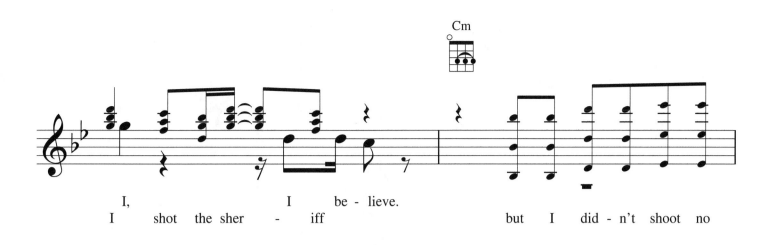

I, shot the sher - iff   I be - lieve.
I shot the sher - iff   but I did - n't shoot no

D.S. al Coda

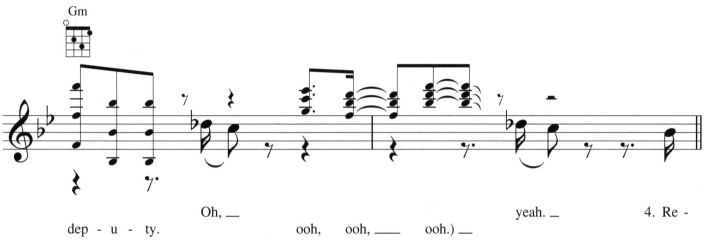

Oh, ___   ooh, ooh, ___ ooh.) ___   yeah. ___   4. Re -
dep - u - ty.

Coda

Begin fade   *Fade out*

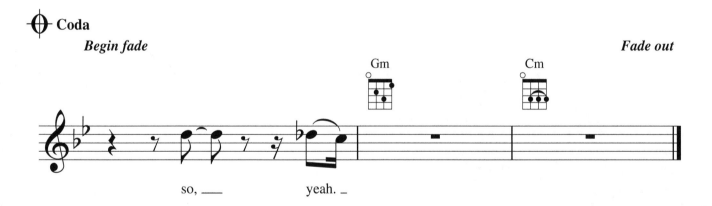

so, ___   yeah. ___

Additional Lyrics

Chorus 2. (I shot the sheriff.) Lord,
            (But I swear it was in self-defense.) Where was the deputy?
            (Oo, oo, oo.) Oo. I say,
            I shot the sheriff.
            But I swear it was in self-defense. Yeah.

Chorus 3. I, I, I, I shot the sheriff.
            Lord, I didn't shoot the deputy. No.
            Yeah, I, I, (Shot the sheriff.)
            But I didn't shoot no deputy. Yeah.

Is This Love
Words and Music by Bob Marley

TRACK 7

Chorus

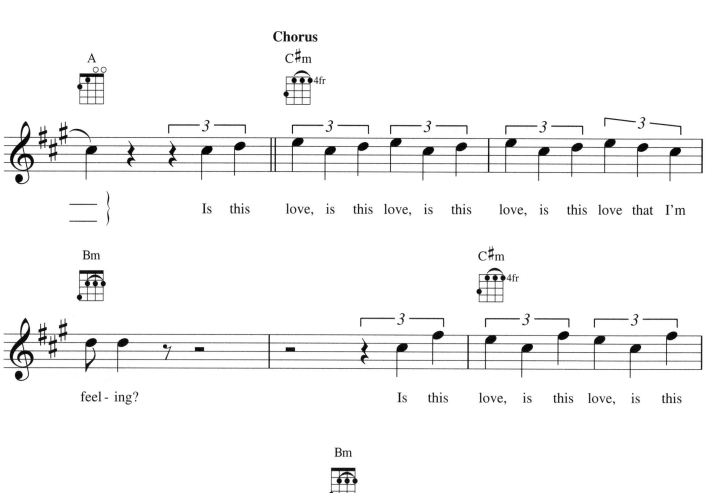

Is this love, is this love, is this love, is this love that I'm feel - ing?

Is this love, is this love, is this

love, is this love that I'm feel - ing?

Bridge

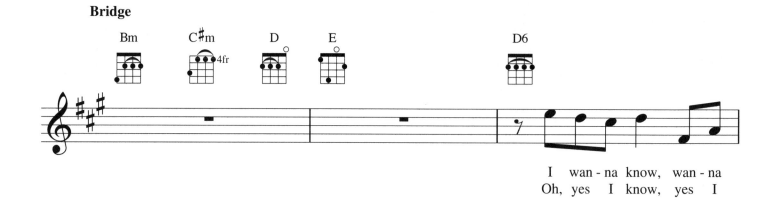

I wan - na know, wan - na
Oh, yes I know, yes I

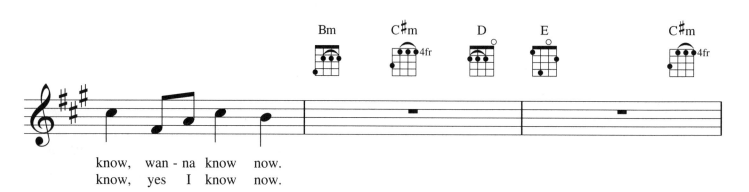

know, wan - na know now.
know, yes I know now.

I've got to know, got to know, got to know, now.
Oh, yes I know, yes I know, yes I know, now.
I _____

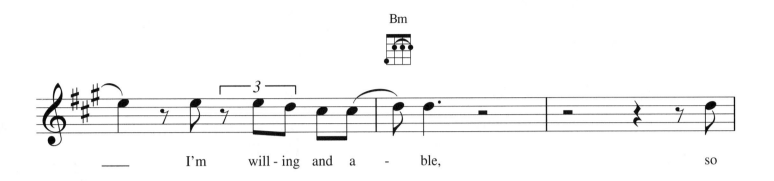

Bm

____ I'm will-ing and a - ble, so

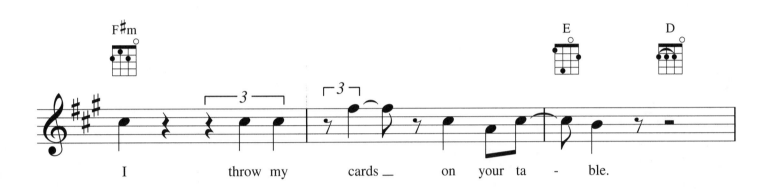

F#m   E   D

I   throw my   cards __ on your ta - ble.

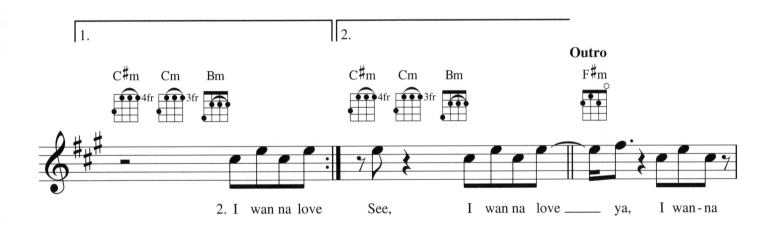

1.   2.   **Outro**

C#m Cm Bm   C#m Cm Bm   F#m

2. I wan na love   See,   I wan na love _____ ya,   I wan-na

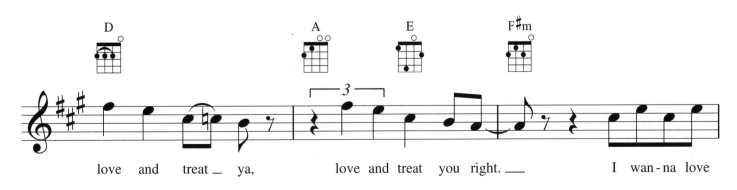

D   A   E   F#m

love and treat _ ya,   love and treat you right. ___   I wan-na love

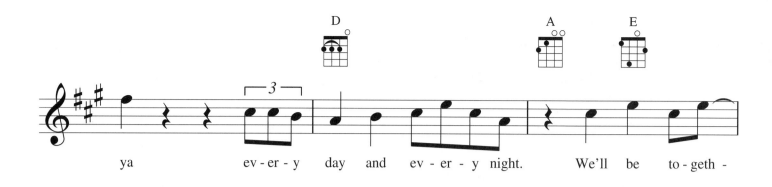

ya   ev - er - y   day   and   ev - er - y   night.   We'll   be   to - geth -

- er   with   the   roof   right   o - ver   our   heads.

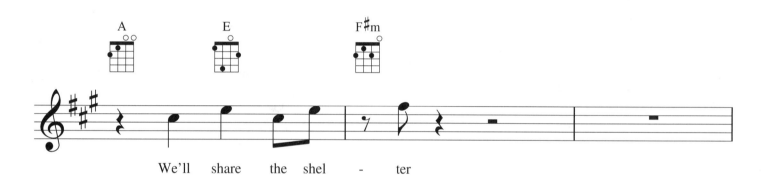

We'll   share   the   shel   -   ter

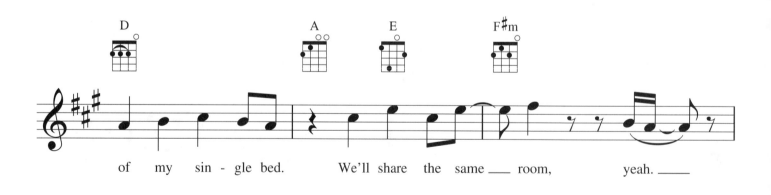

of   my   sin - gle   bed.   We'll   share   the   same ___ room,   yeah. ___

Begin fade   ***Fade out***

Jah   pro - vides   the   bread. ___   We'll   share   the   shel -

No Woman No Cry

Words and Music by Vincent Ford

First note

Intro
Moderately slow ♩ = 78

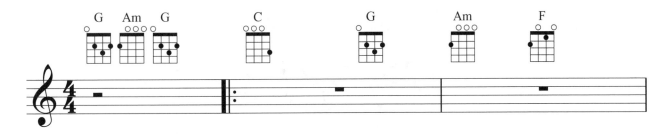

Play 4 times

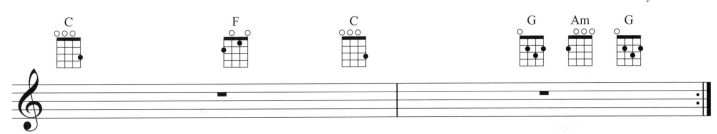

Chorus

No ___ wom - an, no cry. ___
No ___ wom - an, no cry. ___

No wom - an, no cry. ___
No wom - an, no cry. ___

___ No ___ wom - an, ___ no ___ cry.
___ Here, ___ lit - tle dar - lin', don't shed no tears.

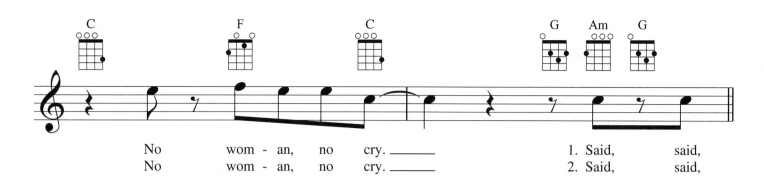

No   wom - an,   no   cry. _____   1. Said,   said,
No   wom - an,   no   cry. _____   2. Said,   said,

𝄋 Verse

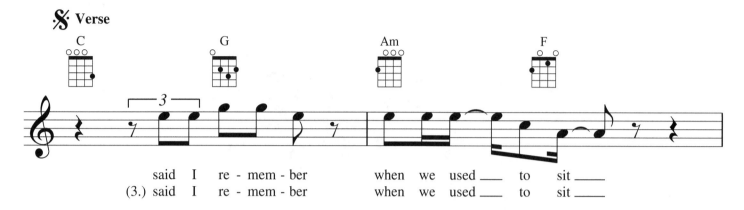

said   I   re - mem - ber   when   we   used ___   to   sit ___
(3.) said   I   re - mem - ber   when   we   used ___   to   sit ___

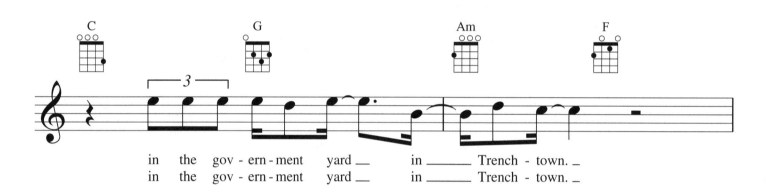

in   the   gov - ern - ment   yard __   in _____ Trench - town. _
in   the   gov - ern - ment   yard __   in _____ Trench - town. _

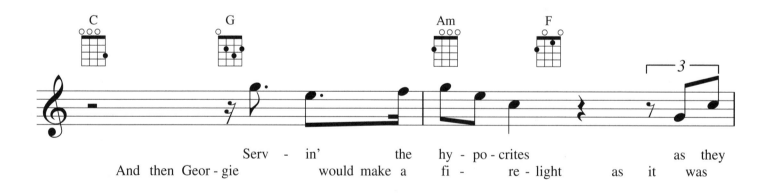

Serv - in'   the   hy - po - crites   as   they
And   then   Geor - gie   would   make   a   fi - re - light   as   it   was

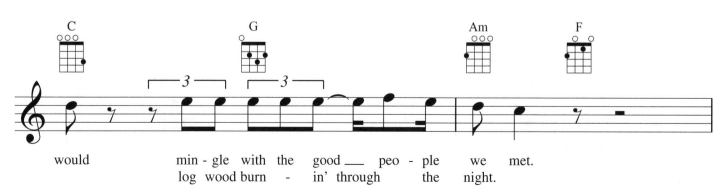

would   min - gle   with   the   good ___ peo - ple   we   met.
log   wood   burn - in' through   the   night.

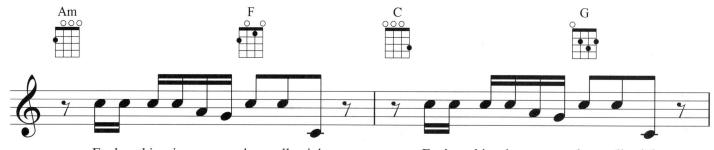

Ev-'ry-thing is gon-na be all right.   Ev-'ry-thing is gon-na be all right.

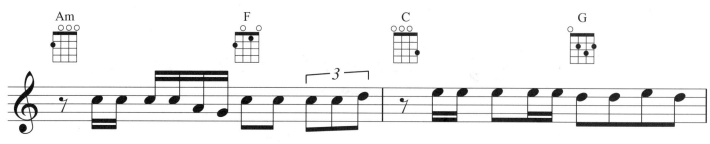

Ev-'ry-thing is gon-na be all right. I say,   ev-'ry-thing's gon-na be all right, ya.

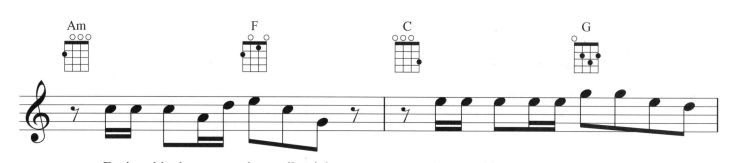

Ev-'ry-thing's gon-na be all right.   Ev-'ry-thing's gon-na be all right, yeah.

Chorus

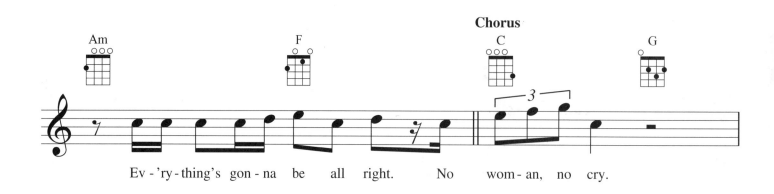

Ev-'ry-thing's gon-na be all right.   No wom-an, no cry.

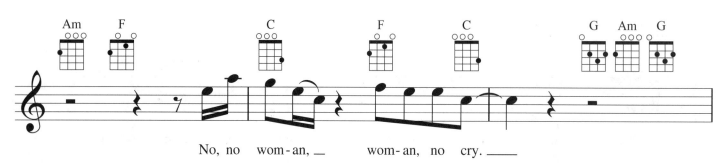

No, no wom-an, __ wom-an, no cry. ___

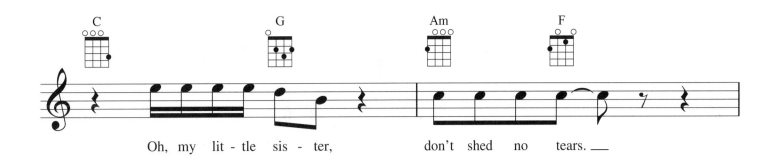

Oh, my lit - tle sis - ter, don't shed no tears. ___

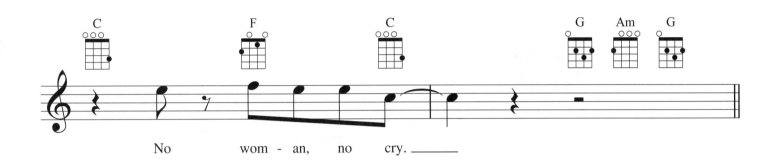

No wom - an, no cry. _____

Guitar Solo

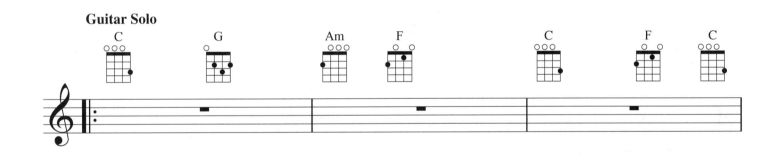

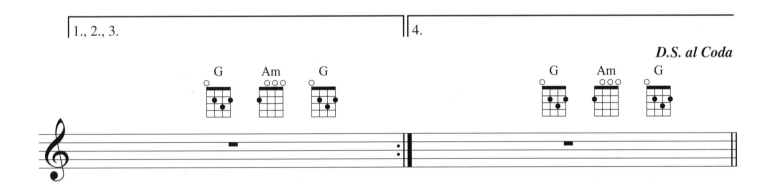

1., 2., 3.

4.

D.S. al Coda

Coda

Chorus

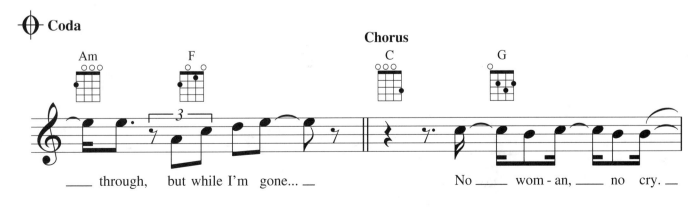

___ through, but while I'm gone... ___

No ___ wom - an, ___ no cry. ___

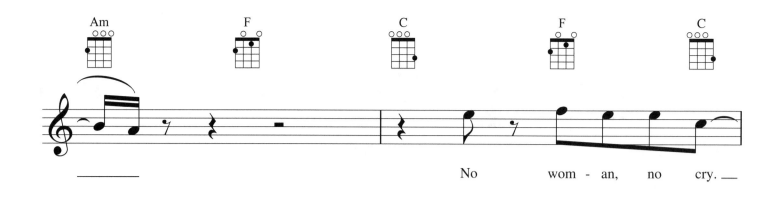

No wom - an, no cry. ___

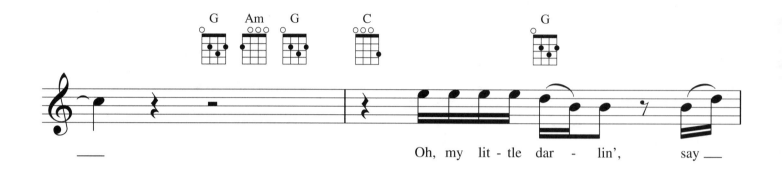

___ Oh, my lit - tle dar - lin', say ___

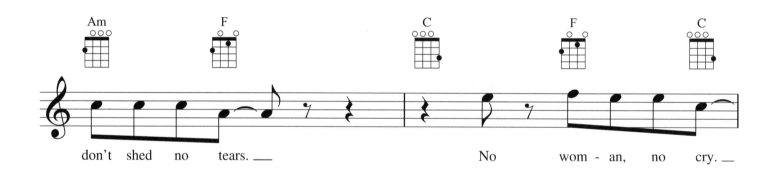

don't shed no tears. ___ No wom - an, no cry. ___

Outro-Chorus

___ Yeah. (Lit - tle dar - lin',

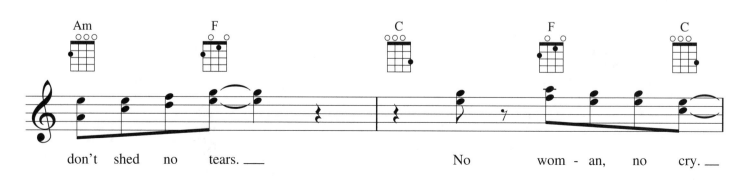

don't shed no tears. ___ No wom - an, no cry. ___

Lit - tle sis - ter,

don't shed no tears. ___   No   wom - an,   no   cry.) __

___

Jamming

Words and Music by Bob Marley

TRACK 9

First note

Intro

Moderately ♩ = 124 (♪♪ = ♩♪)

Half-time Reggae feel

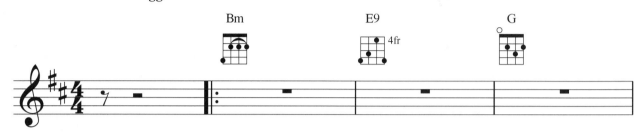

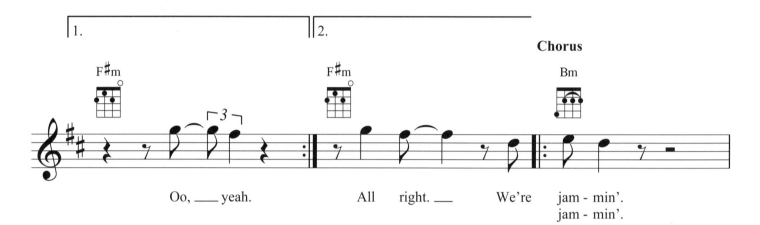

Oo, ___ yeah.　　　All right. ___　We're jam - min'.
　　　　　　　　　　　　　　　　　　　jam - min'.

I wan - na jam it with you. ___　　　　We're
To think that jam-min' was a thing of the past. ___　　We're

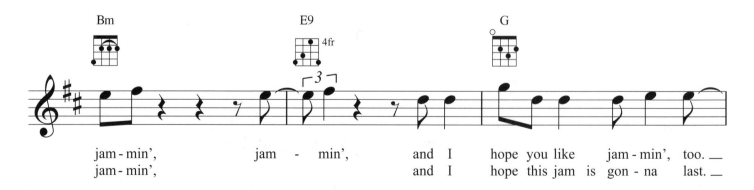

jam - min',　　jam - min',　and I hope you like jam - min', too. ___
jam - min',　　　　　　　and I hope this jam is gon - na last. ___

Stir It Up

Words and Music by Bob Marley

Verse

a long, _ long time   since I've _ got you _ on my _
2. I'll push the wood and I'll   blaze the fire. _____
3. Quench me   when I'm thirst - y.

_____ mind. _   Whoa.   Mm. _ And
Then I'll sat - is - fy your   heart's de - sire.
Come on cool me down, ba - by,   when I'm hot.

now _ you are here. _   I _____ say it's so clear _____ to
Said I'll stir _ it,   yeah,   ev - 'ry min - ute,
Your rec - i - pe,   dar - ling,   is so tast - y,

see _ what uh, we will do, ba - by.   Just _ me and _ you. Come on and
all you've _ got to do, ba - by,   is keep it in it and
and you sure   can stir your pot. So

Chorus

stir _ it up,   I _____ wan - na say,   lit - tle dar - ling, yeah.
stir _ it up,   come on _____   lit - tle dar - ling,
stir _ it up,   oh,   lit - tle dar - ling,

35

TRACK 15

Three Little Birds

Words and Music by Bob Marley

First note

Intro
Moderately slow ♩ = 74

Chorus

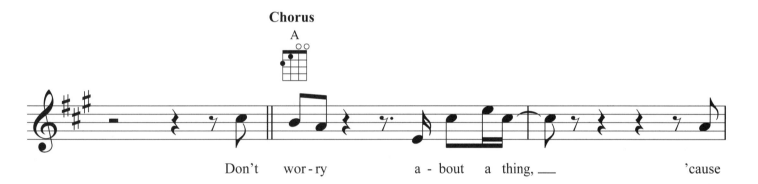

Don't wor-ry a-bout a thing, ___ 'cause

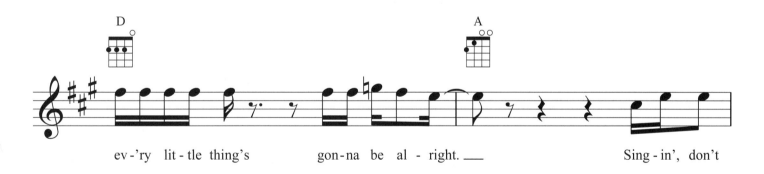

ev-'ry lit-tle thing's gon-na be al-right. ___ Sing-in', don't

wor-ry a-bout a thing, ___ 'cause

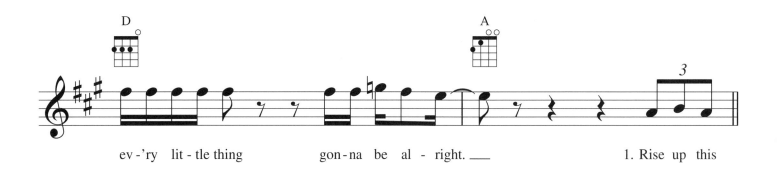

ev -'ry lit - tle thing   gon - na be al - right. __   1. Rise up this

Verse

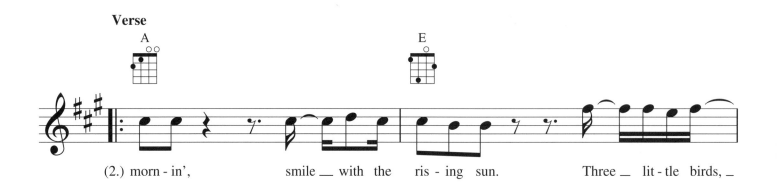

(2.) morn - in',   smile __ with the ris - ing sun.   Three __ lit - tle birds, __

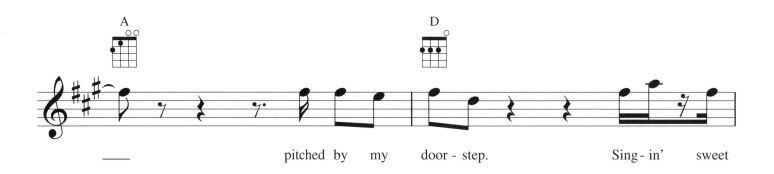

__   pitched by my door - step.   Sing - in' sweet

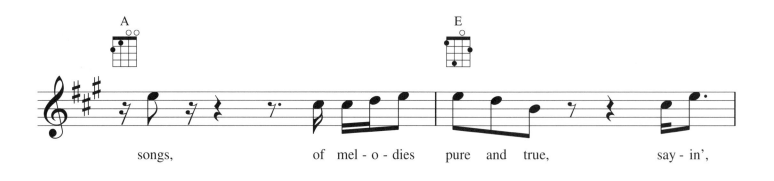

songs,   of mel - o - dies pure and true,   say - in',

"This is my mes - sage to you, whoo, hoo."   Sing - in', don't

Chorus

wor - ry   a - bout   a   thing, ___   'cause

ev - 'ry   lit - tle thing   is gon - na be al - right. ___   Sing - in', don't

wor - ry,   don't wor - ry 'bout   a   thing, ___   'cause

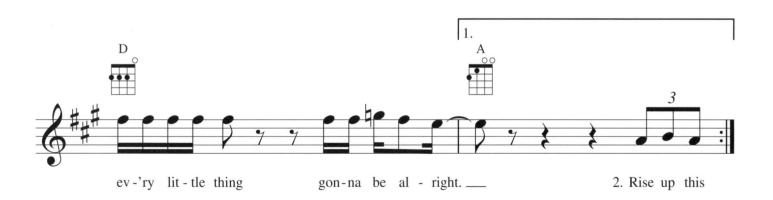

1.

ev - 'ry   lit - tle thing   gon - na be al - right. ___   2. Rise up this

2.

Chorus

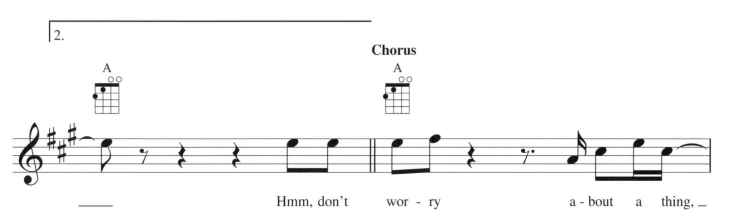

___   Hmm, don't   wor - ry   a - bout a thing, ___

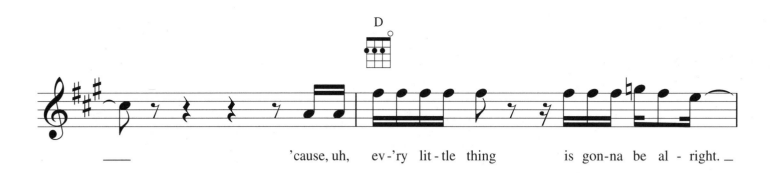

'cause, uh, ev-'ry lit-tle thing   is gon-na be al - right. _

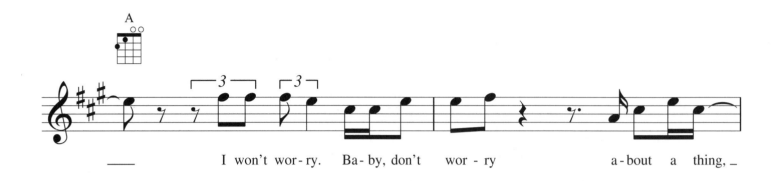

_   I won't wor-ry. Ba-by, don't wor - ry   a-bout a thing, _

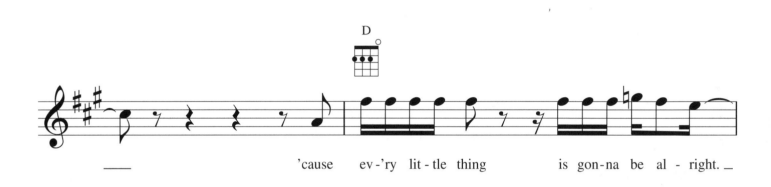

_   'cause ev-'ry lit-tle thing   is gon-na be al - right. _

Begin fade

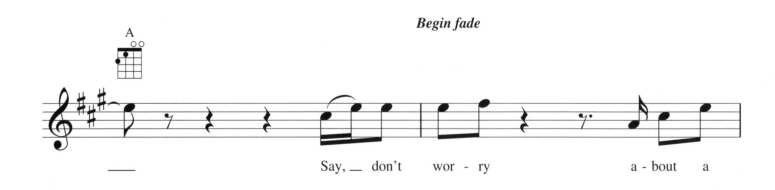

_   Say, _ don't wor - ry   a - bout a

Fade out

thing, no girl, _   'cause ev-'ry lit-tle thing   is gon-na be al - right. _